CARE PLANS IN
REALITY

THE NURSE'S HELPING HAND

Debion White RN

AuthorHouse™ UK
1663 Liberty Drive
Bloomington, IN 47403 USA
www.authorhouse.co.uk
Phone: 0800.197.4150

Published by AuthorHouse 01/27/2016

ISBN: 978-1-5049-9861-1 (sc)
ISBN: 978-1-5049-9862-8 (hc)
ISBN: 978-1-5049-9863-5 (e)

Contents

Acknowledgements

Many thanks to my previous colleagues who offered positive comments about the standard of these care plans and those that have kept samples for their Nursing and Midwifery Council (NMC) Revalidation. I would also like to thank Dona for her ongoing positive feedback and my immediate family members for their ongoing support.

Care Plans in Reality

On most occasions when writing care plans for our patients we would focus on including the twelve activities of daily living, along with other relevant care plans to address the care needs of our patients, if we are using the Roper Logan and Tierney model of nursing. However, for the purpose of this book the care plans are not focused on one patient and they are not signed and dated.

This book is focused on the following patients:

1. Jack Barnes is a gentleman who has been prescribed regular medication.

2. Hilda Vine is a lady whose bedroom is located on the ground floor. She would require assistance to safety in the event of a fire. She is unable to walk but is able to move around independently in her wheelchair. She transfers from bed to chair and vice versa with two staff members' assistance.

3. Tom has a history of falls, mobilises independently but has an unsteady gait. Tom does not wish to use any mobility aid at present due to his current mental health status. Tom also wears glasses.

4. Heather experiences difficulty expressing her needs. She does not have any hearing problems at present but wears glasses.

5. Edward has a medical history of asthma and is at risk of experiencing shortness of breath.

6. Carol has been prescribed Glyceryl Trinitrate (GTN) for chest pain.

7. Pauletta was found by the postman in an unkempt condition. Pauletta was admitted to hospital and was diagnosed with vascular dementia. Pauletta has been admitted into our care home. Pauletta has no family.

8. James has a past medical history of recurrent seizures.

9. Stan has a history of stroke.

10. Loretta has a medical history of Type 1 diabetes. She has been prescribed insulin.

11. Monica was admitted to the home with a low Body Mass Index (BMI).

12. Thomas' consultant, after various examinations and follow-up appointments has instructed for Thomas to have a long-term catheter due to Thomas' urological problems.

13. Velda experiences urine and faecal (double) incontinence and is dependent on staff members to anticipate and maintain these needs.

14. Due to Iris' current physical and mental health deficits she is dependent on two staff members to anticipate and assist her in maintaining her personal cleansing and dressing needs.

15. Arthur is unable to indicate to staff if he is feeling hot or cold due to his current health conditions.

16. Robert is unable to walk or transfer himself. Robert requires at least two staff members to assist him in transferring safely.

17. Gilbert requires assistance to maintain healthy skin integrity due to being immobile, doubly incontinent and having fragile skin.

18. Audreline is at risk of becoming isolated or bored and requires the input of others to ensure that she enjoys the activities that she likes.

19. Leonard is at risk of not having his desired self image maintained.

20. Carol may experience problems sleeping due to history of being prescribed night sedation

21. Nick requires staff members to provide the care and support that will be required at the end stages of his life.

Maintaining a Safe Environment

Jack Barnes is a gentleman who has been having regular prescribed medication.

Care Plan:	Medication
Name of Service User:	Jack Barnes
Date of Birth:	01.12.55
Bedroom Number:	12

Assessed Risk:	**Goals:**
Due to Jack's current mental health status, he is unable to safely manage his own medication. He requires trained staff members to safely administer his medication.	• To administer Jack's medication in-line with policies, procedures and guidelines. • To maintain Jack's safety. • To maintain some form of independence. • To liaise with GP for medication reviews.

Knowledge and Interventions:

- Jack's history indicates no known allergies.

- Jack has dementia but is able to respond to his name and remembers his date of birth.

- He also has a picture with his medication charts as means of further identification.

- His medication charts are printed with his name, date of birth, no known allergies, time that his medications are due, dosage…

- With his medication charts are copies of the most recent prescription sheets with the doctor's signatures.

The following are a list of Jack's current prescribed medication, indications and some side-effects:

- Amlodipine 5mg tablet in the morning. Amlodipine is used to treat hypertension or as a prophylaxis of angina. Some of the side-effects may include headache, flushing, dizziness, weight changes, dry mouth, gastrointestinal disturbances...

- Atorvastatin 10mg tablet at night. Atorvastatin is used to treat high cholesterol when diets and other measures have failed. It minimises the risk of cardiovascular events. Some of the side-effects of Atorvastatin may include weight gain, blurred vision; pain (chest, back, neck)...

- Citalopram 20mg tablet in the mornings. Citalopram is used to treat depressive illnesses or panic disorders. Some of the side-effects may include coughing, yawning, confusion, aggression, abnormal dreams...

- Folic acid 5mg tablet in the morning. Folic Acid is used to treat folate deficient megaloblastic anaemia. Side-effects are rare but may include gastrointestinal disturbances.

- Metformin 500mg tablet in the morning and at 17:00 hours. Metformin is used to treat diabetes mellitus. Some side-effects may include nausea, vomiting, diarrhoea, abdominal pain, taste disturbances; decrease B12 absorption...

Interventions:

- Trained staff members are to administer Jack's medication as prescribed (checking prescription sheet against printed medication chart) by ensuring that necessary safety checks such as the 5 rights of medication administration (right patient, right drug, right dose, right route, right time) are undertaken.

- Trained staff members are to communicate with Jack during medication administration to ensure his understanding of indications, the importance of taking his medication and also in gaining his consent and concordance.

- To maintain some form of independence especially as Jack is able to put his own medication in his mouth and drinks independently once he is given a drink. To take into account that Jack likes to drink water with his medication. He will also sit in an upright posture to take his medication.

- Trained staff members are to liaise with Jack's doctor to ensure that his medication reviews are up-to-date.

- To also seek earlier doctor's review of Jack's medication if side-effects are observed.

- To also refer to the British National Formulary, pharmacist... for further information.

- To carry out evaluations of this care plan on a monthly basis and as often as required e.g. discontinuation or refusal of medication etc.

Care Plan Completed by (Print and sign name): ....

....

Date Completed: ....

Time Completed: ....

Service User's Signature (this is evidence that the care plan was discussed and agreed):

....

Maintaining a Safe Environment

Hilda Vine is unable to walk. She is able to transfer from bed to chair and vice versa. She is also able to mobilise independently with the aid of her wheelchair. Her bedroom is located on the ground floor. Hilda would require help to safety in the event of a fire.

Care Plan:	Fire Evacuation
Name of Service User:	Hilda Vine
Date of Birth:	11.02.56
Bedroom Number:	26

Assessed Risk:	**Goals:**
Hilda is at risk of becoming seriously injured in the event of a fire.	<ul><li>To maintain Hilda's safety in the event of a fire.</li><li>To work in-line with policies and procedures and preserve lives.</li></ul>

Knowledge and Interventions:

- Hilda is unable to walk but is able to transfer herself from bed to chair and vice versa. She is also able to mobilise independently in her wheelchair from one area to the other. Hilda's bedroom is located on the ground floor.

Implementations:

- All staff members on duty should work in accordance with the agreed Personal Emergency Evacuation Plan to ensure their safety, Hilda's safety and the safety of others.

- All staff members should be aware of the fire assembly point. Fire alarms should be tested on a weekly basis. Staff members should be assessed for effectiveness during fire drills.

- Staff members should alert the fire and rescue services, if there is a fire, giving full necessary details and ensure that a senior person is nominated to meet the team when they arrive.

- Staff members are to follow instructions given by fire Marshall/fire officer to ensure safe evacuation.

- In the event of a fire if Hilda is on the first or second floor, staff members should not encourage Hilda to take the lift due to the risk of being trapped as a result of possible electrical failure.

- Effective communication and reassurance should be maintained to minimise Hilda's anxieties and in ensuring safe evacuation.

- During evacuation at least two competent individuals should assist Hilda down the stairs using evacuation equipment if it is safe to do so or assist Hilda to at least two fire doors away from the fire.

- Staff members are to attend mandatory training and other training sessions that are provided. They should also report concerns to management to ensure appropriate actions are taken to maintain a safe environment.

- Responsible staff members are to review and update Hilda's risk assessment, care plan and evaluation as often as necessary or on a monthly basis.

Care Plan Completed by (Print and sign name): ....

....

Date Completed: ....

Time Completed: ....

Service User's Signature (this is evidence that the care plan was discussed and agreed):

....

Maintaining a Safe Environment

Tom has a history of falls, mobilises independently but has an unsteady gait. Tom does not wish to use any mobility aid at present due to his current mental health status. Tom also wears glasses.

Care Plan:	Risk of falls
Name of Service User:	Tom Greegly
Date of Birth:	15.08.1958
Bedroom Number:	2

Assessed Risk:	**Goals:**
Tom has an unsteady gait and a history of falls. He is at risk of falling.	• To maintain Tom's independence. • To maintain a safe environment for Tom. • For Tom to be involved with other members of the multidisciplinary team to ensure optimum care is provided for him. • For Tom to be actively involved in his care and for his choices to be respected.

Knowledge and Interventions:

- Tom mobilises independently but has an unsteady gait.

- Tom stated that he fell in the past.

- His medical history also indicates that he has a history of falls.

- Tom does not wish to use any mobility aid at present.

- Tom also wears glasses.

Implementations:

- Staff members are to prompt Tom to ensure that his glasses are clean and intact and liaise with Tom's optician if Tom is experiencing difficulty seeing whilst utilising his glasses.

- Tom stated that he will use the call bell at nights if he is experiencing difficulty and this has been confirmed by staff members. Staff members are to ensure that Tom's call buzzers are in perfect working order and maintenance, nurse-on-duty and management should be informed if his buzzers are not working properly.

- Tom is currently not keen on having a commode at his bedside at nights as he prefers to walk to his en suite bathroom which also has an emergency call buzzer.

- He has given consent for staff members to carry out hourly checks at nights as long as he is not being disturbed. He also sleeps with his small night light. Staff members are to ensure that checks are undertaken quietly and safely and concerns with noisy doors reported to maintenance and nurse-on-duty.

- Staff members are to maintain a safe environment at all times e.g. by ensuring that floors are free from obstacles; wet floor signs are used immediately after seeing a spillage, monitoring area and cleaning up spillages appropriately (using wet and dry mop...) and promptly.

- Handrails are to be well-fitted and nurse-on-duty, maintenance and management informed promptly of faults. In maintaining safety the 'out-of-use' sign should be utilised until the area is safe.

- To also promptly remove obstacles and maintain a clutter free environment.

- To ensure that an up-to-date record of Tom's blood pressure is maintained and concerns reported to Tom's doctor.

- The doctor should also be informed if Tom is experiencing pain or discomfort or problems to his skin integrity which might result in further compromise to his mobility.

- If Tom experiences a fall to the floor, staff members should be trained in using safe moving and handling techniques to assist Tom off the floor safely; if it is safe to move Tom following assessment for injuries and if Tom is struggling to get up on his own.

- Staff members should only move Tom if it is safe e.g. if Tom is able to do most of the work himself and only requires minimal assistance.

- If suspected broken limb is considered following assessment then Tom's comfort should be maintained as much as possible whilst on the floor until the emergency team arrives as moving Tom could result in further injuries.

- Trained staff members are to take into account Tom's wishes in regards to hospital admission.

- Assessment results indicate that Tom would require a medium sling (write the colour) to be transferred with using the hoist (write the name of the hoist). Safety checks should be undertaken to ensure that equipment is safe to use.

- If assessment indicates that Tom has seriously injured himself e.g. head injury, broken bones, dislocation of joints... The ambulance should be summoned and Tom should be kept as comfortable as possible whilst maintaining his privacy and dignity. A record should be made of his vital signs.

- A falls diary should be maintained if Tom falls and Falls team's input should be requested for recurrent falls.

- Next-of-kin should be made aware of the incident.

- Relevant documentation such as body mapping, incident report, updating care plan, care plan evaluation, risk assessment, daily notes, professional visitor's record, relative's communication sheet... should be carried out by staff members as soon as possible after event.

- To ensure active involvement of other members of the multidisciplinary team as needed to ensure optimum care is provided for Tom.

- To evaluate Tom's care plan on a monthly basis and as often as possible to ensure that additional measures are put in place if required to maintain optimum care for Tom.

Care Plan Completed by (Print and sign name): ....

....

Date Completed: ....

Time Completed: ....

Service User's Signature (this is evidence that the care plan was discussed and agreed):

....

Communication

Heather wears glasses; does not demonstrate any problems hearing but experiences difficulty expressing her needs on occasions.

Care Plan:	Communication
Name of Service User:	Heather Green
Date of Birth:	11.02.65

Bedroom Number:	9

Assessed Risk:	Goals:
Heather experiences difficulty expressing her needs verbally, resulting in barriers to communication.	• For staff members to communicate with Heather effectively. • To understand Heather's needs and maintain these needs with Heather's consent. • To develop a therapeutic relationship with Heather. • To promote interaction and minimise the risk of Heather becoming isolated. • For staff to liaise with other members of the multidisciplinary team whilst demonstrating respect for Heather's choices, wishes or decisions.

Knowledge and Interventions:

- Heather experiences difficulty expressing her needs. She does not have any hearing problems at present but wears glasses.

Implementations:

- Staff members are to develop a trusting therapeutic relationship with Heather and ensure effective communication is maintained at all times.

- To ensure Heather's understanding and in gaining her consent to maintain her care needs in a dignified and respectful manner.

- Good eye contact (without staring), body posture and facial expression should be maintained at all times during interaction with Heather and Heather should be allowed to express herself without interruption.

- Staff members could consider the environment e.g. interacting with Heather in a quiet area away from distractions with good room lighting, speaking at a moderate pace, not shouting, using good facial expression, good body language and speaking in simple terms...

- Staff members are to communicate with Heather in a respectful manner at all times to gain full insight into Heather's perspective, situation, feelings, concerns, needs...

- To clarify Heather's concerns with Heather to ensure clear understanding.

- To ensure that appropriate actions are taken to maintain optimum individualised care for Heather.

- To keep Heather informed of actions taken to relieve her concerns.

- Currently Heather demonstrates the ability to hear quite well. However, if Heather starts expressing concerns with her ears or hearing then doctor/General Practitioner (GP) should be contacted, with Heather's consent and GP's recommendations maintained.

- Heather has been accepting the Optician's review of her eyes on a yearly basis. However, staff members are to liaise with the optician if Heather is experiencing difficulty with her eyes or glasses.

- To promote interaction and prompt Heather to become actively involved in her activities of daily living including social activities with the activities' coordinators to minimise the risk of Heather becoming isolated.

- For staff to liaise with other members of the multidisciplinary team whilst demonstrating respect for Heather's choices, wishes or decisions and in ensuring optimum care is provided for Heather.

- Responsible staff members are to review and update Heather's care plan and evaluation as often as necessary or on a monthly basis.

Care Plan Completed by (Print and sign name): ....

....

Date Completed: ....

Time Completed: ....

Service User's Signature (this is evidence that the care plan was discussed and agreed):

....

SECTION

3

Breathing and Circulation

Edward has a medical history of asthma and is at risk of experiencing shortness of breath.

Care Plan:	Asthma
Name of Service User:	Edward Leeds
Date of Birth:	31.03.1954
Bedroom Number:	1

Assessed Risk:	**Goals:**
Edward has a medical history of asthma and is at risk of experiencing shortness of breath.	• To encourage Edward to maintain good inhaler techniques. • To administer treatment as prescribed and in-line with policies and procedures. • To liaise with other members of the multidisciplinary team. • To demonstrate respect for Edwards choices, privacy and dignity.

Knowledge and Interventions:

- Edward has been actively involved with GP and Practice nurse to ensure appropriate review, assessment and treatment is provided for Edward.

- Edward is at risk of becoming breathless. Edward has been prescribed Salbutamol inhaler when required and has a spacer device.

- Trained staff members are to ensure that if Edward's symptoms are getting worse that Edward's Salbutamol inhaler is administered to help in getting his asthma back under control.

- If Edward's symptoms are more severe, the usual dose of Salbutamol should be administered straight away with the use of his spacer device.

- Edward should be encouraged to keep calm and relaxed as much as his condition allows.

- Staff members are to stay calm and reassuring and ensure the room that Edward is in is well ventilated.

- Edward should be encouraged to sit in an upright position to encourage maximum lung expansion.

- Edward could be encouraged to sit in an upright position whilst resting his arms comfortably on a table with cushion in front of him to minimise the risk of Edward becoming more exhausted.

- Edward's symptoms tend to be relieved with his Salbutamol inhaler after five to ten minutes.

- If Edward's inhaler is not having any effect e.g. if Edward is unable to complete sentences in one breath, too breathless to speak, bradycardia..., then Edwards GP should be contacted and depending on how severe Edwards's condition is getting then the ambulance should be summoned (999). Trained staff members should assess Edward's vital signs including oxygen saturation levels (normal ranges could be included e.g. blood pressure 120 mmHg/80mmHg).

- Edward should be encouraged to take his Salbutamol until help arrives.

- Staff members are to ensure that Edward's confidentiality, privacy and dignity are maintained at all times and next of kin informed.

- All concerns and actions taken are to be reported, recorded and documented to ensure optimum care is provided for Edward.

Care Plan Completed by (Print and sign name): ....

....

Date Completed: ....

Time Completed: ....

Service User's Signature (this is evidence that the care plan was discussed and agreed):

....

Breathing and Circulation

Carol has been prescribed Glyceryl Trinitrate (GTN) for chest pain.

Care Plan:	Chest Pain – Angina
Name of Service User:	Carol Chance
Date of Birth:	02.1.59
Bedroom Number:	19

Assessed Risk:	Goals:
Carol has been prescribed Glyceryl Trinitrate (GTN) for chest pain	• To administer treatment as prescribed. • To maintain Carol's comfort, privacy, dignity and independence • To monitor vital signs weekly and when required • To liaise with GP and other members of the team

Knowledge and Interventions:

- Carol is currently able to inform staff members of chest discomfort.

- Carol tends to use the nurse call buzzer to gain assistance with her care needs and has been empowered to inform staff members of her needs by using the nurse call buzzer as appropriate, to alert staff members if she is experiencing chest discomfort. However, staff members are aware of the need to maintain regular checks to ensure that Carol is comfortable.

- Carol has been prescribed GTN spray (which may cause side-effects such as postural hypotension, tachycardia, throbbing, headache, dizziness, nausea, vomiting, heartburn, flushing…) to relieve her angina pain.

- Symptoms of Angina may include: Severe pain in the chest radiating to neck, jaw, and arm (usually left). The pain could be described as squeezing, crushing or gripping pain. Carol is also at risk of getting breathless on exertion, anxious or may experience pain in other areas.

- To administer Carol's GTN spray as prescribed and appropriately (e.g. encouraging Carol to have her GTN spayed under her tongue, allowing five minutes between each spray - **maximum of three sprays)** to relieve her angina pain.

- To monitor Carol's vital signs (blood pressure, pulse rate and rhythm, oxygen saturation…), encourage Carol to rest and offer reassurance and support to minimise her anxieties. Carol's confidentiality, privacy and dignity should be maintained at all times.

- If Carol's angina worsens, occurs on minimal exertion or at rest or nocturnal, is more frequent and with persistent pain that last longer than fifteen minutes then the ambulance (999) should be summoned as Carol would be at high risk of myocardial infarction (MI)/heart attack.

- Staff members are to develop a therapeutic relationship with Carol to gain some understanding of precipitating factors, that may cause Carol to start experiencing pain e.g. exertion, stress, eating large meals, cold weather…

- To work with Carol to minimise the risks of identified precipitating factors resulting in her experience of chest discomfort.

- To encourage Carol to eat healthily whilst respecting her choices and decisions at all times.

- To provide health promotions and liaise with other members of the multidisciplinary team with Carol's consent to ensure safe and efficient care is provided for Carol.

- To keep Carol's GP updated on concerns, maintain GP's recommendations and liaise with GP for general health and medication reviews in a timely manner.

- All concerns and actions should be reported, recorded and documented.

Care Plan Completed by (Print and sign name): ....

....

Date Completed: ....

Time Completed: ....

Service User's Signature (this is evidence that the care plan was discussed and agreed):

....

Care Plan:	Vascular Dementia
Name of Service User:	Pauletta Jones
Date of Birth:	01.1.55
Bedroom Number:	5a

Assessed Risk:	**Goals:**
Pauletta was found by the postman in an unkempt condition. Pauletta was admitted to hospital and was diagnosed with vascular dementia. Pauletta has been admitted into our care home. Pauletta has no family.	▪ To ensure that Pauletta is orientated as much as possible into the home environment. ▪ For staff members to develop a therapeutic relationship with Pauletta. ▪ To act in Pauletta's best interest. ▪ To demonstrate respect for Pauletta's privacy and dignity. ▪ To liaise with other members of the multi-disciplinary team to ensure optimum care is provided for Pauletta. ▪ To administer treatment as prescribed and in-line with policies, procedures and guidelines.

Knowledge and Interventions:

- Vascular Dementia is caused by brain damage from cerebrovascular or cardiovascular problems and can also be a result of genetic diseases. Vascular Dementia is a common form of dementia resulting from an impaired supply of blood to the brain causing cognitive impairment associated with gradual death of brain cells.

- Pauletta is currently demonstrating a decline in her ability to remember recent events, difficulty finding words, becoming tearful; unable to plan or maintain her activities of daily living which are some of the experiences that individuals with vascular Dementia experience.

- Pauletta has a close friend who brought some pictures of Pauletta when Pauletta was younger. One of the pictures showed Pauletta on the beach and another showed Pauletta walking up a hill in a knitted top. Pauletta's friend stated that she could remember when Pauletta knitted the top that she wore in the picture. Pauletta's friend also stated that she met Pauletta at the theatre.

- Pauletta has been assigned a named nurse and a named carer who are planning to work together to put as much information and pictures together to make a folder about Pauletta.

- Pauletta's friend stated that she would like to be actively involved in making up the folder about Pauletta and indicated that she would take some more pictures to the home on her next visit.

- Staff members are to ensure that a good, trusting therapeutic relationship is developed and maintained with Pauletta and her friend.

- Staff members are to encourage Pauletta to be actively involved in making up the folder e.g. by encouraging Pauletta to stick some of her photographs into the folder and talking with her about them.

- During Pauletta's mental capacity assessment Pauletta demonstrated no insight into the care and treatment that she requires.

- Pauletta is unable to express her needs verbally and requires staff members to use effective communication in a calm and reassuring manner to ensure that Pauletta's needs are maintained whilst working in Pauletta's best interest.

- Pauletta seems to get tearful in noisy environments and likes to spend time in the quiet room with sensory lights and relaxing music playing at low volume.

- Pauletta's named nurse is currently liaising with Pauletta's social worker to arrange the input of The Independent Mental Capacity Advocate (IMCA) Service.

- To ensure that contact details for all members of the multidisciplinary team are clearly documented in Pauletta's notes to ensure safe and efficient care is provided for Pauletta.

- The home manager has completed the Deprivation of Liberty Safeguards (DOLS) Form for Authorisation.

- Staff members are to maintain effective communication e.g. reporting, recording, documenting and sharing information within the team about experiences with Pauletta to ensure optimum care is provided for Pauletta.

Care Plan Completed by (Print and sign name): ....

....

Date Completed: ....

Time Completed: ....

Service User's Signature (this is evidence that the care plan was discussed and agreed):

....

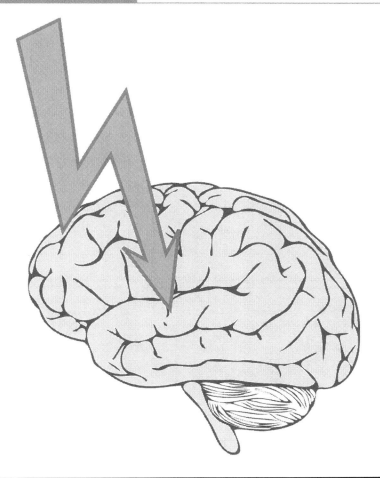

Care Plan:	Seizure
Name of Service User:	James Barnes
Date of Birth:	01.12.55
Bedroom Number:	1

Assessed Risk:	Goals:
James has a past medical history of recurrent seizures.	• For staff members to identify concerns and liaise with GP. • To administer treatment as prescribed. • To maintain James' comfort, privacy and dignity.

Knowledge and Interventions:

- James has been prescribed Sodium Valproate twice a day which is used for the treatment of his seizures.

- Trained staff members are to ensure that James' medication is administered as prescribed and in line with policies and procedures. James' medication should be administered in a timely manner.

- Staff members are to liaise with James' GP if James starts experiencing regular seizures for medication review or further investigation to be carried out to ensure safe and efficient care is provided for James.

- James tends to experience jerky movements and unawareness of what is going on around him.

- James is at risk of having a fall to the floor when he is having a seizure.

- On rare occasions James will complain of headache which is followed by a seizure.

- His communication tends to be less clear.

- Staff members should alert the nurse by pressing the emergency call buzzer.

- This gives staff member's time to assist James into a wheelchair, then straight into his bedroom onto his bed.

- Staff members should not gather around James when he is having a seizure and a cushion should be placed under his head.

- Staff members should allow James' seizure to take its course.

- Staff members should not hold James to stop the seizure or place anything in his mouth.

- James' GP has prescribed rectal diazepam which is to be administered as first line treatment during his seizure.

- Rectal diazepam should be witnessed and administered to James if James' seizure is lasting longer than five minutes as per e.g. GP's recommendation.

- Once seizure has stopped (if James has not been taken off to hospital) staff members should remain calm and reassuring, maintain James' comfort, assist James in the recovery position, ensuring that James' airway is not compromised and his breathing is stable.

- James should be allowed to rest and a staff member should monitor James closely.

- Food and drink should only be offered once James has recovered and fully oriented.

- A record of James' seizure should be maintained.

- Staff members are to report, record and document concerns and actions taken to ensure safe and efficient care is maintained for James.

Care Plan Completed by (Print and sign name): ....

....

Date Completed: ....

Time Completed: ....

Service User's Signature (this is evidence that the care plan was discussed and agreed):

....

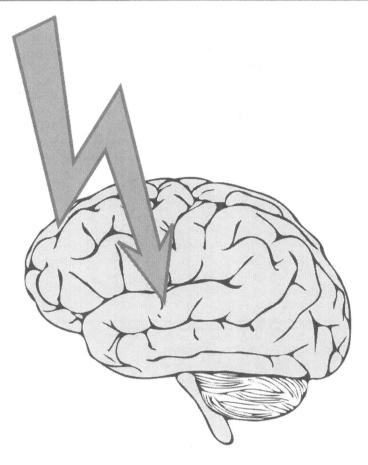

Care Plan:	Stroke
Name of Service User:	Stan James
Date of Birth:	01.2.45
Bedroom Number:	12

Assessed Risk:	**Goals:**
Stan has a history of stroke.	• For staff members to identify concerns and liaise with GP. • To ensure safe and efficient care is provided for Stan. • To administer treatment as prescribed. • To maintain Stan's comfort, privacy and dignity.

Knowledge and Interventions:

Staff members are to observe Stan for the following and summon medical intervention promptly:

- Face- Stan's face may have fallen on one side, Stan may not be able to smile or his mouth or eye may be drooped.

- Arms- Stan may not be able to raise his arms and keep them there because of arm weakness or numbness.

- Speech- Stan's speech may be slurred.

- Time- if Stan experiences the above then the ambulance should be summoned immediately.

Other signs and symptoms may include:

- Dizziness

- Communication problems, difficulty talking and understanding what others are saying

- Problems with balance or coordination which could be difficult to identify considering Stan already has this problem. Therefore staff members are to get to know Stan as this will help in identifying changes.

- Difficulty swallowing

- Severe headaches

- Numbness or weakness resulting in complete paralysis of one side of the body

- Loss of consciousness

Staff members are to press the emergency buzzer to gain the nurse's prompt input if the nurse is not in sight.

- To maintain effective communication with Stan at all times and offer reassurance and support in a calm and reassuring manner to minimise his anxieties.

- To keep next of kin updated on concerns and actions taken.

- To evaluate care plan on a monthly basis and as often as necessary.

Care Plan Completed by (Print and sign name): ....

....

Date Completed: ....

Time Completed: ....

Service User's Signature (this is evidence that the care plan was discussed and agreed):

....

Eating and drinking

Loretta has a medical history of Type 1 diabetes. She has been prescribed insulin.

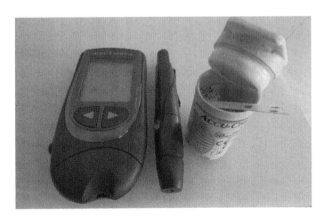

Care Plan:	Type 1 diabetes mellitus
Name of Service User:	Loretta Aston
Date of Birth:	06.06.59

Bedroom Number:	7
Assessed Risk: Loretta has a medical history of Type 1 diabetes. She has been prescribed insulin.	**Goals:** • To gain Loretta's consent to care. • To promote Loretta's education. • To maintain good diabetic care and control and near normal blood glucose levels. • To alleviate symptoms, minimise complications. • To ensure regular GP reviews and access to other members of the multidisciplinary team including podiatrist, dietician, diabetic nurse ...

Knowledge and Interventions:

- Loretta requires trained staff members to prompt her to have her blood glucose levels checked (name the machine and equipments utilised to check blood glucose levels) before insulin (name the insulin and dose prescribed) is administered and when she is feeling unwell.

- Trained staff members are to ensure that Loretta's fingers are cleaned prior to checking her blood glucose levels to minimise the risk of false readings.

- Trained staff members are to liaise with GP and specialist nurses with Loretta's involvement and consent to ensure that there is an agreed aim of the blood glucose level that needs to be maintained for Loretta. Target levels could be between 4-7 mmol/L before meals and under 9 mmol/L two hours after meals.

- Trained staff members are to ensure rotation of injection site; daily thoroughly checks of feet and liaising with care staff after Loretta's personal cleansing and dressing needs are maintained to ensure that any concerns relating to Loretta's skin integrity is dealt with promptly. The involvement of the podiatrist should be requested on a regular basis to ensure optimum care is provided for Loretta.

- Care staff members are to ensure that during assistance with Loretta's cleansing that water temperature is maintained between 41°C - 43°C. Skin care should be maintained and all areas of Loretta's skin should be suitably dried and emollient applied as prescribed. All changes to Loretta's skin condition should be reported to the nurse on duty as soon as possible who will undertake relevant assessments, documentation and referrals to ensure care is maintained to minimise further compromise to Loretta's skin integrity.

- Loretta should be encouraged to wear comfortable footwear and ensuring that socks are not too tight.

- The dentist should also be actively involved in Loretta's care with Loretta's consent as problems with teeth, gums; tongue... could lead to ulceration, discomfort resulting in problems such as poor intake which may cause complications such as hypoglycaemia.

- If Loretta experiences episodes of low blood glucose levels, GP should be informed and GP's recommendation followed. Glucogel should be administered as prescribed. Extra fluids and dietary intake e.g. 50-100mls Lucozade maintained (if Loretta is fully conscious). Loretta's next meal could include bread, potato, pasta, ice cream...

- Trained staff members should be fully trained in assessing Loretta's condition and in ringing 999 for emergency treatment.

- Trained staff members are to ensure strict monitoring of Loretta's input and if blood glucose levels are above accepted range then Loretta's urine sample should be checked and GP informed of concerns. Effective communication should be maintained with Loretta at all times to ensure her understanding of her care needs and actions that are required to ensure her safety.

- Trained staff members are to ensure that care and kitchen staff members are aware of the need for Loretta to eat healthily e.g. maintaining a diet low in saturated fat, salt, increased fruits, vegetable, fibres, lean meats, oily fish…

- Trained staff members are to monitor Loretta's blood pressure on a monthly basis and when required. The aim is to maintain Loretta's blood pressure within acceptable ranges (e.g. less than 135/85 mmHG and above 90/60 mmHg. GP should be informed of high readings. Urine output, colour, frequency, pain when passing urine… should also be taken into account and GP informed of concerns.

- Loretta should be prompted to be actively involved with the activities coordinators to ensure personal physical activities are encouraged.

- Loretta's weight should be checked on a monthly basis and aim for a normal BMI. The dietician's involvement should be requested as needed to ensure optimum care is provided for Loretta.

- Due to Loretta having diabetes she is at risk of developing complications with her eyesight and should be encouraged to have the optician's input in her care (mostly done on a yearly basis).

- Trained staff members are to ensure that close multidisciplinary working is undertaken e.g. liaising with GP for blood test and developing action plans to ensure suitable control.

- Loretta should be empowered to be actively involved in her care and treatment and all concerns should be reported, recorded and documented to ensure quality care is provided for Loretta.

Care Plan Completed by (Print and sign name): ....

....

Date Completed: ....

Time Completed: ....

Service User's Signature (this is evidence that the care plan was discussed and agreed):

....

Eating and drinking

Monica was admitted to the home with a low BMI.

Long term and short term goals could be included in this care plan (see suggestions below):

- The short term goal could be to liaise with the place where Monica was discharged from to find out if Monica was prescribed supplements;

- Liaise with GP promptly to inform him/her of Monica's BMI as there is a possibility that the GP could ensure that supplements are prescribed as soon as necessary;

- The short term goal could be to maintain a strict dietary chart for a week whilst ensuring that referrals are made to relevant members of the team;

- The long term goal could be to maintain Monica's current weight e.g. if Monica's BMI increases to 20.5, which is within the acceptable BMI range.

Care Plan:	Low BMI
Name of Service User:	Monica Sterling
Date of Birth:	08.08.1963
Bedroom Number:	8

Assessed Risk:	**Goals:**
Monica was admitted to the home with a BMI of 17.5 (normal range is 18.5-24.9).	<ul><li>To promote a healthy dietary intake.</li><li>To achieve and maintain an acceptable BMI.</li><li>To liaise with GP and dietician to ensure optimum care is provided for Monica.</li></ul>

Knowledge and Interventions:

- Staff members are to develop a trusting therapeutic relationship with Monica; use effective communication with Monica at all times and demonstrate respect for her choices and wishes.

- Monica is aware of her weight and has agreed for other members of the multidisciplinary team to be actively involved in her care.

- Monica has been informed that a high calorie dietary intake would be beneficial. Monica informed staff members that she likes most food. Monica stated that she likes porridge, toast with jam and a cup of tea in the mornings and a full English breakfast on occasions. Monica also stated that she likes a cooked dinner each day, a light meal at tea time and a snack before retiring to bed.

- Effective communication skills were utilised and Monica agreed to have cream in her creamed potatoes, custards and puddings and full fat/ skimmed milk powder in her cups of teas with a few biscuits.

- Monica was oriented to the home and stated that she would like to have her main meals in the dining room, unless she is unwell.

- Staff members are to ensure that Monica is given the opportunity to have her choice of menu on a daily basis.

- Monica's choices have been taken into account and kitchen staff members have been informed.

- Monica is now on a food chart to ensure her dietary intake is monitored closely.

- Monica has agreed to have her weight monitored on a weekly basis for a month which will then be reduced to monthly once her BMI is within acceptable range.

- Staff members are to ensure that Monica's food chart is kept updated and check Monica's weight on a weekly basis with her consent.

- Trained staff members are to ensure that Monica's MUST (Malnutrition Universal Screening Tool) score and care plan is updated and evaluated (e.g. by including the dietician's / GP's recommendation – which could be collecting blood forms for Monica's blood test to be taken ...) as her needs change.

- Trained staff members are to ensure that GP is aware of Monica's weight and dietician's referral completed.

- Staff members are to ensure that Monica's choices are respected.

- To report, record and document concerns and actions taken to ensure optimum care for Monica.

Care Plan Completed by (Print and sign name): ....

....

Date Completed: ....

Time Completed: ....

Service User's Signature (this is evidence that the care plan was discussed and agreed):

....

Elimination

Thomas' consultant would like Thomas to continue having a long term catheter.

Care Plan:	Thomas has a long term catheter
Name of Service User:	Thomas Chance
Date of Birth:	19.05.60
Bedroom Number:	17

Assessed Risk:	**Goals:**
Thomas' consultant, after various examinations and follow-up has instructed for Thomas to have long-term catheter due to Thomas' urological problems.	• To ensure safe catheter care. • To ensure safe catheterisation in a timely basis. • To minimise the risk of infections. • To communicate effectively with Thomas at all times, gain his consent and demonstrate respect for his choices and decisions. • To maintain Thomas' comfort, privacy and dignity. • To liaise with other members of the multidisciplinary team.

Knowledge and Interventions:

- Thomas has been experiencing bladder retention for sometime now; trial without catheter has been unsuccessful. Thomas' consultant has suggested long-term catheter.

- Thomas has no known allergies at present but his history indicates that Thomas wears a size 14CH catheter as a smaller size tends to bypass.

- Trained staff members are to ensure that the appropriate size catheter is used to minimise the risk of complications and preventable re-catheterisation.

- Thomas will require re-catheterisation on an eleven to twelve weeks' basis and trained staff members are to ensure that this is done in a timely basis.

- Thomas should be kept updated of the date when his catheter is due to be changed. Effective communication should be utilised at all times to ensure Thomas' understanding, to gain his consent and in offering reassurance and support.

- Trained staff members are to ensure that all equipment such as: Catheterisation packs, Catheter, Lignocaine gel, Cleaning solution, Sterile gloves, Catheter bag, 10ml syringe and 10ml sterile water (if not in catheter pack) and Inco pad, urine test strips… are in stock.

- Staff members are to ensure that effective hand hygiene and aseptic technique is utilised at all times throughout the procedure.

- Trained staff members are to ensure that the meatus area is cleaned as per training and guidelines.

- Staff members are to maintain good infection control at all times e.g. decontaminating hands and wearing a new pair of clean, non-sterile gloves before emptying or changing leg bag and cleaning hands after removing gloves. Regular emptying should be maintained to minimise reflux. Urinary bags should always be positioned below the level of the bladder and should not touch the floor.

- Staff members are to ensure that fluid balance chart is maintained at all times to ensure closer monitoring and in identifying concerns (e.g. low input/ output, colour ...).

- Thomas drinks well at present but requires staff members to prompt him to have a drink.

- Staff members are to ensure appropriate investigations are undertaken if concerns arise e.g. if urine is dark, cloudy, smells offensive; pain when passing urine, increased confusion, temperature...

- GP should be informed of concerns and observations' results to ensure safe and efficient care is provided for Thomas.

- Multidisciplinary working should be practiced to ensure optimal care for Thomas.

- Thomas' privacy and dignity should be maintained at all times.

- Full documentation should be maintained after re-catheterisation and all concerns should be reported, recorded, documented and care plan evaluated.

Care Plan Completed by (Print and sign name): ....

....

Date Completed: ....

Time Completed: ....

Service User's Signature (this is evidence that the care plan was discussed and agreed):

....

Elimination

Velda experiences incontinence and is dependent on staff members
to anticipate and assist her in maintaining these needs.

Care Plan:	Incontinence
Name of Service User:	Velda Jones
Date of Birth:	11.11.57
Bedroom Number:	22

Assessed Risk:	**Goals:**
Velda experiences double incontinence. She is dependent on staff members to anticipate and assist her in maintaining these needs.	• To use effective communication with Velda at all times to ensure her understanding and to gain her consent. • To maintain Velda's privacy, dignity and independence at all times. • To liaise with GP and other members of the multidisciplinary team to ensure optimum care is provided for Velda. • To communicate with Velda in a respectful manner whilst demonstrating respect for her choices, privacy and dignity. • To maintain Velda's comfort.

<u>Knowledge and Interventions:</u>

- Staff members are to communicate with Velda in a respectful manner to ensure her understanding and in gaining her consent prior to interventions.

- Velda likes to sit in communal areas during the daytime and will require staff members to anticipate and maintain her incontinence needs.

- Velda does not like others e.g. other patients, visitors ... knowing when she is going to use the toileting facilities.

- Velda has agreed for staff members to ask her if she would like to go on a little journey, then explaining to her in a quiet area what they would like to assist her with, whilst communicating with her in a respectful and dignified manner.

- Velda utilises a medium size pad (name the pad or company where the pad was made).

- Staff members are to ensure that Velda wears the correct size pads.

- Good infection control is to be maintained at all times by ensuring that gloves and aprons are worn whilst assisting Velda with her incontinence needs. Clinical wastes should be disposed of appropriately e.g. in clinical waste during and soon after intervention. Staff members are to maintain good hand hygiene before and after the intervention.

- Good communication should be maintained at all times during the intervention to encourage compliance and in minimising Velda's anxieties.

- Curtains should be drawn and doors closed to ensure Velda's privacy and dignity is maintained at all times.

- Velda has a barrier cream (name the cream) which she has three times a day. Staff members are to ensure that Velda's barrier cream is applied as prescribed and recorded appropriately e.g. as per policies and procedures.

- Any concerns observed e.g. if Velda's urine is offensive, dark or if her stool is loose, hard, black etc. the nurse-on-duty should be informed who will assess and liaise with GP as appropriate. Trained staff members are to ensure that laxatives are administered as prescribed and in-line with policies and procedures.

- Staff members are to encourage a good fluid intake of at least 1.5 litres per day and a diet high in fibre.

- Velda is immobile and requires staff members to prompt her to be actively involved in activities that are appropriate to her needs.

- All concerns are to be reported, recorded and documented to ensure optimal care is maintained for Velda.

Care Plan Completed by (Print and sign name): ....

....

Date Completed: ....

Time Completed: ....

Service User's Signature (this is evidence that the care plan was discussed and agreed):

....

SECTION 6

Personal Cleansing and Dressing

Due to Iris' current physical and mental health deficits she is dependent on two staff members to anticipate and assist her in maintaining her personal cleansing and dressing needs.

Care Plan:	Personal Cleansing and Dressing
Name of Service User:	Iris Cole

Date of Birth:	28.08.1948
Bedroom Number:	23

Assessed Risk:	**Goals:**
Due to Iris' current physical and mental deficits she is dependent on two staff members to anticipate and assist her in maintaining her personal cleansing and dressing needs.	• To demonstrate respect for Iris' choices, comfort, privacy and dignity. • To encourage Iris to maintain some form of independence. • To maintain Iris' high standard of personal hygiene. • To ensure multidisciplinary team working.

Knowledge and Interventions

- Staff members are to ensure that effective communication skills are maintained at all times in a respectful manner to ensure Iris' understanding, in gaining her consent to assist her with maintaining her personal cleansing and dressing needs and to minimise her anxieties.

- A safe environment should be maintained at all times e.g. by identifying potential risks and eliminating hazards.

- All equipment such as Iris' pad, flannel, wipes, towels, shower gel, shampoo, creams, deodorant, gloves, aprons... should be gathered prior to the intervention and with Iris' involvement.

- Iris should be given the opportunity to choose suitable clothing that will maintain a comfortable body temperature for her.

- Iris likes to have a shower at least three times per week and a full body wash on other occasions. Staff members are to ensure that Iris is offered a choice and her choice should be respected.

- If Iris chooses to have a shower then the bathroom should be safe e.g. shower chair should be in good working order, water temperature (not exceeding 41°C for showering and regular checking should be maintained during shower to identify changes to water temperature that would warrant suspension of the intervention to ensure Iris' safety) should be checked with thermometer and temperature recorded.

- If Iris chooses to have a full body wash water temperature should not exceed 44°C and should be comfortable for Iris.

- S.F. (maintenance manager) undertakes routine maintenance and should be informed immediately if concerns with equipment arise. The nurse-on-duty and home manager should be made aware. Temporary out-of-use sign should be used if concerns arise to ensure a safe environment is maintained at all times.

- Once all safety checks are undertaken bathroom door should be closed and curtains drawn to ensure Iris' privacy and dignity are maintained.

- During the intervention, staff members are to ensure that Iris' body temperature is maintained e.g. by covering areas such as Iris' back, legs… as appropriate if those areas are not being tended to at that very minute.

- Iris is able to wash and dry her face, arms, abdomen and the top of her thighs with prompting and supervision. Staff members are to ensure that Iris' independence is maintained and Iris is assisted with other areas that are hard for her to reach.

- During personal cleansing close attention should be maintained to identify any compromise to Iris' skin integrity such as discolouration, swelling, scratches, wounds, dry scalp, bad teeth…

- A body mapping should be completed and the nurse informed of any concerns. The nurse will then carry out the nursing process to ensure safe and efficient care is provided for Iris.

- Iris has been prescribed emollient (name the emollient) to keep her skin moist and a barrier cream to protect bony prominences. Staff members are to ensure that Iris' skin is thoroughly patted dry and creams applied as prescribed (a record could be made on TMARS - topical medication administration record sheet).

- Iris is also able to brush her teeth after tooth paste has been applied to her toothbrush and requires prompting and supervision. The nurse should be informed of any concerns observed during oral care and the input of the dentist requested or GP's consultation requested.

- Staff members are to ensure that close attention is paid to Iris' nails and chiropodist input requested as needed.

- Iris struggles to put her clothes on and requires assistance from staff members. Iris is able to lean forward, lean back or lift her legs.

- Staff members should ensure that Iris is left safe and comfortable after the intervention and laundry and clinical waste dealt with appropriately.

- All concerns should be reported, recorded and documented to ensure optimal care is provided for Iris.

- This care plan (also refer to risk assessment) should be updated, evaluated on a monthly basis and when required.

Care Plan Completed by (Print and sign name): ....

....

Date Completed: ....

Time Completed: ....

Service User's Signature (this is evidence that the care plan was discussed and agreed):

....

Controlling Body Temperature

Arthur is unable to indicate to staff if he is feeling hot or cold due to his current health conditions.

Care Plan:	Controlling Body Temperature
Name of Service User:	Mr. Arthur White
Date of Birth:	20.03.1924
Bedroom Number:	1

Assessed Risk:	Goals:
Arthur is unable to indicate to staff if he is feeling hot or cold due to his current health conditions.	■ To anticipate and maintain a comfortable body temperature for Arthur. ■ To maintain Arthur's comfort, privacy and dignity at all times. ■ To ensure Arthur's safety.

Knowledge and Interventions:

- Staff members are to ensure that effective communication skills are utilised at all times to ensure Arthur understands and in gaining his consent.

- Arthur is chair bound and is dependent on staff members to assist him with his activities of daily living.

- Arthur likes to use his duvet cover when in bed at nights and likes to be covered with a light blanket in the daytime when he goes for a nap.

- Staff members are to ensure that faults with the heating system are reported to the manager promptly and maintenance staff informed.

- To encourage Arthur to dress warm when the weather is cold and reduced clothing during hot weather.

- Radiators should be adjusted, extra blankets and warm drinks should be encouraged (during cold weather) to maintain a body temperature that is comfortable for Arthur. During hot weather extra fluids (particularly cold) should be encouraged to ensure Arthur is kept well hydrated.

- In the summer months Arthur likes to sit in the garden. Arthur should be encouraged to sit in shaded areas and sun screen should be applied with Arthur's consent.

- If Arthur is looking unwell, the nurse on duty should be informed to ensure safe and efficient care is provided for Arthur through the nursing process.

- To liaise with Arthur's next of kin to acquire suitable clothing for Arthur as he requires.

- To ensure monthly and when required care plan update.

Care Plan Completed by (Print and sign name): ....

....

Date Completed: ....

Time Completed: ....

Service User's Signature (this is evidence that the care plan was discussed and agreed):

....

SECTION

8

Mobilising

Robert is unable to walk or transfer himself. Robert requires at least two staff members to assist him in transferring safely.

Care Plan:	Mobility
Name of Service User:	Robert Taylor
Date of Birth:	28.08.1933
Bedroom Number:	2

Assessed Risk:	**Goals:**
Robert is unable to walk or transfer himself. Robert requires at least two staff members to assist him in transferring safely.	<ul><li>To maintain a safe environment for Robert.</li><li>For Robert to be actively involved in his care.</li><li>To demonstrate respect for Robert's choices.</li><li>For Robert to maintain some form of independence.</li><li>For Robert to be involved with other members of the multidisciplinary team to ensure optimum care is provided for him.</li></ul>

Knowledge and Interventions:

- Robert is immobile and is fully dependent on staff members to assist him to transfer safely.

- Robert is able to move in bed with minimal assistance.

Implementations:

- To use effective communication with Robert at all times to ensure his understanding and to gain his consent prior to the intervention.

- To ensure that interaction is maintained at all times before, during and after the intervention.

- To ensure that Robert's general health and presentation are taken into account prior to the intervention. If Robert is looking unwell e.g. being lethargic, cold, sweaty, clammy... The nurse-on-duty should be informed to ensure Robert's safety.

- Robert's risk assessment in-line with his current weight indicates that Robert will require the medium sling (write the name and colour of the sling if possible) and the compatible hoist (write the name of the hoist if possible).

- Up-to-date records of Robert's weight should be maintained in order to identify weight gain or loss and reassessment of his sling and hoist.

- To ensure that the hoist sling is compatible to the hoist, the sling should be the correct size in-line with Robert's weight. The weight limit on the hoist should not be exceeded.

- At least two staff members should assist Robert during this intervention.

- Robert utilises the large red slide sheet which is kept in his top draw in his bedroom.

- Staff members should not use the hoist unless they are trained to do so.

- Robert will require a wheelchair (name of wheelchair, serial number if possible) wheelchair with foot plates for Robert to rest his feet and pressure cushion (write the name of the cushion) to maintain his comfort when he is seated in the wheelchair.

- All equipment should be checked before utilising to ensure that they are well intact and in correct working order. The manufacturer's instructions should be followed and staff should be aware of the emergency lowering system. The date of PAT test should be in date and concerns should be communicated with the manager.

- Staff members are to ensure that the environment is as clutter free as possible enabling sufficient space for the manoeuvre. Brakes should not be utilised during hoisting, batteries should be fully charged and the hoist should only be used for transferring Robert and not as a transport.

- Robert is at risk of becoming vulnerable and as a result each stage of the manoeuvre should be explained to Robert to ensure his understanding and in minimising anxieties. Reassurance should be given to Robert as needed.

- All individuals involved in the manoeuvre should communicate effectively with each other to maintain safety, comfort and in minimising the risk of injuries to Robert and staff members.

- All concerns should be reported to the nurse-on-duty, maintenance, home manager…

- Care plans, care plan evaluation and risk assessment should be updated on a monthly basis and when required.

Care Plan Completed by (Print and sign name): ....

....

Date Completed: ....

Time Completed: ....

Service User's Signature (this is evidence that the care plan was discussed and agreed):

....

Skin Integrity

Gilbert requires assistance to maintain healthy skin integrity due to being immobile, doubly incontinent and having fragile skin.

Care Plan:	Skin Integrity
Name of Service User:	Mr. Gilbert Mullings
Date of Birth:	28.06.1940
Bedroom Number:	3

Assessed Risk:	**Goals:**
Gilbert requires assistance to maintain healthy skin integrity due to being immobile, doubly incontinent and having fragile skin.	• For Gilbert to maintain healthy skin integrity by identifying factors early that might compromise Gilbert's skin. • To liaise with other members of the multidisciplinary team such as GP, Tissue Viability Nurses (TVN), community nurses, dietician as needed to ensure optimum care is provided for Gilbert. • To work in-line with policies and procedures to ensure Gilbert's safety.

Knowledge and Interventions:

- For all staff members to use effective communication with Gilbert at all times to ensure his understanding, minimise his anxieties and in gaining his consent.

- With Gilbert's consent the initial assessment was carried out within six hours of Gilbert being admitted into the home. Gilbert's score indicated that he is at increased risk of developing pressure damage.

- Gilbert's entire body was checked and special attention was paid to his heels, shoulders, back of head, sacrum, scrotum, groin... Gilbert's heels were red but blanching and body mapping chart has been completed.

- Gilbert has been prescribed barrier cream (write the name of the cream) which should be applied to his heels and to other at risk areas e.g. bony prominences.

- Gilbert has been provided with a 'Brand Name' alternating mattress for his profiling bed. The mattress has been set according to Gilbert's weight and in-line with the manufacturer's instructions.

- Gilbert stated that he would like to have his dinner in the dining room.

- Staff members are to ensure that Gilbert is seated comfortably in his wheelchair on his 'Brand Name' pressure cushion and his choices respected. Gilbert is aware of his fragile skin integrity and would like to have his dinner promptly then assisted back to bed after approximately 40 minutes after eating.

- Staff members are to ensure that the hoist sling is not left underneath Gilbert after manoeuvre as this may cause compromise to his skin integrity.

- Staff members are to ensure that safe moving and handling techniques are utilised using the (write the colour) sling and the 'Brand Name hoist. Gilbert has also been provided with his (colour) slide sheets which are to be utilised to minimise shearing and other damage to his skin integrity, during two hourly repositioning and when positioning Gilbert for transfers. Maintenance, manager, nurse-on-duty ... should be informed promptly of any concerns with equipment following appropriate checks prior to the intervention.

- Care should be maintained to ensure that bony prominences are kept from direct contact with each other.

- Gilbert is doubly incontinent and requires staff members to anticipate and maintain his incontinence needs.

- Staff members are to ensure that care is taken when assisting Gilbert with his personal hygiene needs by ensuring that all areas are cleaned appropriately, patted dry; barrier cream applied to affected and at risk areas and his emollient applied to other areas (as indicated on chart) to minimise dry skin. Gilbert's privacy and dignity should be maintained at all times.

- Any concerns observed with Gilbert's skin integrity should be reported immediately to the nurse-on-duty who will undertake full assessment and documentation and liaise with GP as necessary.

- Gilbert's BMI is within range at present. Staff members are to ensure that Gilbert is weighed on a monthly basis and gain advice on nutritional status if concerns arise. Other members of the multidisciplinary team e.g. dietician, tissue viability nurses... should be involved in Gilbert's care if required and with Gilbert's consent.

- All records and documentation should be kept up-to-date and care reviewed on a monthly basis and when required to ensure that optimum individualised care is provided for Gilbert.

Care Plan Completed by (Print and sign name): ....

....

Date Completed: ....

Time Completed: ....

Service User's Signature (this is evidence that the care plan was discussed and agreed):

....

Working and Playing

Audreline is at risk of becoming isolated or bored and requires the input of others to ensure that she enjoys the activities that she likes.

Care Plan:	Social Interaction
Name of Service User:	Mrs. Audreline Taylor
Date of Birth:	28.08.1949
Bedroom Number:	40

Assessed Risk:	**Goals:**
Audreline is at risk of becoming isolated or bored and requires the input of others to ensure that she enjoys the activities that she likes.	• For Audreline to maintain social interaction and stimulation. • For her to be actively involved in the activities of her choice and gain some fulfilment. • To demonstrate respect for her choices, privacy and dignity.

Knowledge and Interventions:

• Audreline likes to receive assistance with her personal cleansing and dressing needs prior to having her breakfast which she has at the dinner table sitting next to Mrs. S and Mr. Y who she seems to be at ease with.

• After breakfast Audreline likes to read her daily newspaper, browse through her magazines, listen to music or watch television.

• Audreline liked baking and gardening in the past and tends to opt for the opportunity to be involved in baking and gardening with the activities coordinator.

- Audreline also liked interior decorating and her daughter stated that Audreline used the old machines with the pedal in the past. Audreline's daughter brought the machine into the home and Audreline tends to like talking about how she used the machine in the past.

- Audreline also liked going shopping, going out for meals or for a cup of tea and cake with friends, going to the park and seeing the ducks. She stated that she used to like going to the theatre on occasion and has been on week-end breaks to the sea side in England.

- Audreline stated that she would enjoy visiting some of these places whilst living in the home.

- Following discussion with Audreline's daughter who is her next-of-kin, she has agreed to take Audreline out shopping on a monthly basis in order for her to choose her clothes. She also stated that she would inform the home of dates when she will be available and was also encouraged to inform staff members of Audreline's experience whilst out.

- The activities coordinator has been informed of Audreline's interests and stated that she will keep a record of the places that Audreline visits after activities and will liaise with the nurse-on-duty to ensure Audreline is appropriately risk assessed for relevant activities.

- Audreline sings and claps during the musician's visits once a month and stated that she likes the entertainment although she gets emotional on occasions.

- She tends to be actively involved in bingo games and also likes to do a bit of knitting on occasions.

- Staff members are to ensure that Audreline is given the opportunity to be fully involved in activities to minimise her risk of feeling bored or isolated and in ensuring optimum care is provided for her.

- Staff members are to maintain good communication with Audreline's family and friends who visit on a regular basis.

- All concerns are to be reported, recorded and documented and regular record should be made of Audreline's involvement in activities.

Care Plan Completed by (Print and sign name): ....

....

Date Completed: ....

Time Completed: ....

Service User's Signature (this is evidence that the care plan was discussed and agreed):

....

SECTION 10

Expressing sexuality

Leonard is at risk of not having his desired self image maintained.

Care Plan:	Self Image
Name of Service User:	Leonard Chance
Date of Birth:	01.01.1953
Bedroom Number:	45

Assessed Risk:	Goals:
Leonard is at risk of not having his desired self image maintained.	• For all staff members to demonstrate respect for Leonard's self image. • To offer assistance and support to Leonard to ensure that his self image is maintained.

Knowledge and Interventions:

• Leonard likes to wear his skirt, blouse, brazier, stockings, make-up, wig and perfume on Fridays and stated that he has been doing this since he was 58 years old after loosing his wife to cancer.

• Leonard's family thinks it's his way of coping with the loss of his wife. His daughter stated that she only found out a few years ago and Leonard isolated himself as he thought his family would not understand.

• Staff members are to ensure that Leonard's choices are respected and assistance given to Leonard as needed. Leonard is able to put most of his clothes on but struggles with his stockings and make-up.

• Leonard's daughter is actively involved in ensuring that Leonard has sufficient make-up and clothing but requires staff members to keep her informed if Leonard requires a new wig, stockings etc.

- Leonard likes to get dressed up on Friday afternoons and would like staff members to assist him to his bedroom. After dressing up Leonard likes to stay in his bedroom for the rest of the evening. He also likes a small glass of wine whilst watching some of the programmes that he would enjoy watching with his wife when she was alive.

- On other days of the week Leonard likes to look presentable in appearance.

- He likes to have a shave on alternate days during assistance with his personal cleansing and dressing needs. He likes to use his aftershave.

- Leonard likes to wear his vest, shirt, jumper, pants, trousers, socks and his shoes.

- Leonard does not like when his clothes is soiled with food after meals and will require staff members to assist him to be changed into clean clothing.

- Staff members are to report, record and document concerns and actions taken to ensure optimum patient-centred care is maintained for Leonard.

Care Plan Completed by (Print and sign name): ....

....

Date Completed: ....

Time Completed: ....

Service User's Signature (this is evidence that the care plan was discussed and agreed):

....

Sleeping

Carol may experience problems sleeping due to history of being prescribed night sedation

Care Plan:	Sleeping
Name of Service User:	Carol Chance
Date of Birth:	01.1.57
Bedroom Number:	11

Assessed Risk:	**Goals:**
Carol may experience problems sleeping due to history of being prescribed night sedation.	• For Carol to have restorative sleep. • To demonstrate respect for Carol's choices and decisions. • To maintain Carol's safety, comfort and dignity. • To ensure multidisciplinary team working as needed.

Knowledge and Interventions:

• Carol is immobile and requires two staff members to assist her into bed by 19:00hours as she likes to watch her TV programmes. Carol likes a cup of hot chocolate, crackers and cheese or a couple slices of toasts while watching her programmes. She also likes a glass of water on her bedside table in order for her to have sips when she is awake.

• Carol likes to have a light wash and change into her night dress of her choice before retiring to bed.

- Carol likes her bedroom door closed to maintain her privacy and dignity at all times. Staff members should ensure that Carol's bedroom door is closed after checks (Carol has agreed to have staff members check on her while she is asleep but would like this to be done quietly without waking her).

- Carol sleeps on a 'brand name' mattress and does not utilize bedrails at present.

- Carol likes to have only one pillow as she stated in the past that she is able to adjust her profiling bed to maintain her comfort.

- Carol also likes her cushion at the bottom of the bed to prevent her feet touching the bottom of the bed.

- Carol likes to cover with her sheet and duvet cover.

- Carol is able to press the call buzzer at nights to gain assistance with her toileting needs.

- Staff members are to ensure that any concerns identified with Carol's call buzzer is reported promptly.

- Carol likes to sit at the dining table in the mornings (between 07:30hours and 08:30hours) for breakfast after being assisted with her personal cleansing and dressing needs.

- Trained staff members are to carryout risk assessments and update Carol's care plan if her needs change.

- Trained staff members are to gain GP's involvement if Carol starts experiencing problems sleeping.

- Staff members are to ensure that noisy doors are reported to the nurse on duty, manager, maintenance etc to minimise disruptions.

- All concerns should be reported to the nurse on duty to ensure optimum care is provided.

Care Plan Completed by (Print and sign name): ....

....

Date Completed: ....

Time Completed: ....

Service User's Signature (this is evidence that the care plan was discussed and agreed):

....

Death and dying

Nick requires staff members to provide the care and support that will be required at the end stages of his life.

Care Plan	End Stages of Life
Name of Service User	Nick Cage
Date of Birth	18.12.21
Bedroom Number	1

Assessed Risk:	**Goals:**
Nick requires staff members to provide the care and support that will be required at the end stages of his life.	▪ To administer treatment as prescribed that will maintain Nick's comfort.
	▪ To demonstrate respect for Nick's wishes, privacy and dignity.
	▪ To offer information and support to Nick and his family.
	▪ To ensure optimum care is provided for Nick at all times and during the end stages of life and after death.

Knowledge and Interventions:

- Nick is currently not for resuscitation; his condition is stable at present. Nick has been eating, drinking and concordant with his regular medication as prescribed by GP

- Staff members are required to be vigilant in recognising when Nick's condition is deteriorating and liaise with GP whilst maintaining effective communication with Nick and his family members as per his choice.

- Staff members are to take into account reversible causes of Nick being unwell e.g. infection, dehydration might be possible then consent to treatment should be gained and discussions maintained about the outcome e.g. benefits or risks.

- To ensure that respect is demonstrated for Nick's needs and wishes and that they are reviewed and revised on a regular basis.

- Staff members are to ensure that all communication (e.g. about goals and treatments) with Nick and his loved ones are undertaken in a sensitive manner to relieve further anxieties during end of life care.

- To ensure that Nick and his friends and loved ones (those important to Nick) are allowed to be actively involved in Nick's care as much as Nick would like and increased reassurance and support offered as necessary.

- To ensure that the needs of Nick's family are identified and support is given as required. Staff members should achieve this by making time to talk with Nick and his loved ones. If death is expected then the goals (e.g. to maintain Nick's comfort) should be communicated with Nick and significant others.

- Nick's family should be well supported and aware of the nurse call buzzer to gain assistance as needed. Nick's family should also be offered refreshments, leaflets, GP contacts…

- Trained staff members are to ensure that Nick's care plans are kept up to date as soon as possible after changes have been made e.g. if GP has discontinued medications that are no longer beneficial to Nick or if alternative medications have been prescribed e.g. if Nick is experiencing increased difficulty swallowing and GP has prescribed medication via the subcutaneous or transdermal routes.

- Trained staff members are to take into account symptoms to address e.g. pain, shortness of breath, nausea, vomiting, confusion, restlessness, urinary retention, dry mouth, respiratory secretions… and liaise with GP and manager to ensure that all necessary treatment and equipment (e.g. nebulizer, suction machine, syringe driver…) are available to ensure optimum care is provided for Nick.

- To be aware of some possible signs that death may occur. It may be that GP need to be contacted promptly because Nick is taking hardly any food, only managing sips of fluids, having difficulty with oral medication, becoming increasingly weak, spending more time asleep, difficulty responding, not responding to treatment, Nick feeling that he is going to die…

- To ensure that Nick is supported with food and fluids by mouth as long as it is tolerated and safe to do so bearing in mind that a reduced need for food and fluids is part of the dying process.

- To ensure that last offices is undertaken with dignity and respect for choices and wishes are maintained in-line with policies and procedures.

- Good infection control should also be maintained in-line with policies and procedures.

Relevant details that might be beneficial

- Name of first and second contact:
- Telephone Numbers:
- Time when contact can be made:
- Nick's Relationship to contacts:
- Professionals' contact e.g. GP, district/Palliative care nurses, Independent Mental Capacity Advocate, social worker, Deprivation of Liberty Safeguards, Care Quality Commission (CQC), Coroner…

- Name and contact details of spiritual advisors:
- Faith: Nick was an active member of the local Anglican Church and enjoys the visits from the Bishop.
- Beliefs: Nick believes that there is life after death and stated that he would like friends from his local church to visit him during the end stages of his life.
- Feelings: Nick also stated that his family members are not very religious and thinks that it would be best if arrangements are made in advance.
- Wishes: Nick has a cross and his bible which he would like to be placed on his bed.
- Funeral Directors: [write the name and contact details of Funeral directors]
- Burial/Cremation: Nick would like to be buried.
- To ensure that all relevant professionals involved in Nick's care is informed of death and outstanding appointments cancelled.

- To liaise with management for further information e.g. if post-mortem is required, notification to coroner, CQC...

- To ensure that significant others are aware of how to get Nick's death certificate and in contacting Nick's chosen funeral directors.

- To ensure that equipment are returned as soon as possible for cleaning etc.

Care Plan Completed by (Print and sign name): ....

....

Date Completed: ....

Time Completed: ....

Service User's Signature (this is evidence that the care plan was discussed and agreed):

....

Further information can be gathered from:

Alzeimer's Society. (2016). *Deprivation of Liberty Safeguards (DoLS)*. Available: https://www.alzheimers.org.uk/site/scripts/documents_info.php?documentID=1327. Last accessed 15ᵗʰ January 2016.

Amanda Gordon. (March 2015). *The Seventh Year of the Independent Mental Capacity (IMCA) Service* . Available: https://www.gov.uk/government/uploads/system/uploads/attachment_data/file/416341/imca-report.pdf. Last accessed 15ᵗʰ January 2016.

Asthma UK. (July 2015). Asthma Attacks. Available: https://www.asthma.org.uk/advice/asthma-attacks/. Last accessed 12ᵗʰ January 2016.

Blood Pressure UK. (2008). What is normal blood pressure?. Available: http://www.bloodpressureuk.org/BloodPressureandyou/Thebasics/Whatisnormal. Last accessed 12ᵗʰ January 2016.

British Heart Foundation. (2015). Angina. Available: https://www.bhf.org.uk/heart-health/conditions/angina. Last accessed 12ᵗʰ January 2016.

British National Formulary. (2014). *DIAZEPAM*. Available: http://www.evidence.nhs.uk/formulary/bnf/current/4-central-nervous-system/41-hypnotics-and-anxiolytics/412-anxiolytics/benzodiazepines/diazepam#PHP2160. Last accessed 15ᵗʰ January 2016.

British National Formulary. (2014). *SODIUM VALPROATE*. Available: http://www.evidence.nhs.uk/formulary/bnf/current/4-central-nervous-system/48-antiepileptic-drugs/481-control-of-the-epilepsies/valproate/sodium-valproate. Last accessed 15ᵗʰ January 2016.

Cardinal Stritch University Library. (2016). *Roper, Logan & Tierney - Elements of Nursing*. Available: http://www.stritch.edu/Library/ Doing-Research/Research-by-Subject/Health-Sciences-Nursing-Theorists/Roper,-Logan---Tierney---Elements-of-Nursing/. Last accessed 26th January 2016.

Care Commission. (2008). Promoting nutrition in care homes for older people. Available: http://www.dignityincare.org.uk/_library/ Resources/Dignity/CSIPComment/promotingnutritionincare_ homes1.pdf. Last accessed 12th January 2016.

Diabetes UK. (2016). Testing. Available: https://www.diabetes.org. uk/Guide-to-diabetes/Monitoring/Testing/#glucose. Last accessed 12th January 2016.

Dignity In Care. (2012). Respecting dignity. Available: http://www. dignityincare.org.uk/Resources/Respecting_dignity/. Last accessed 12th January 2016.

Fire Safety Advice Centre. (2015). Fire Emergency Evacuation Plan and the Fire Procedure. Available: http://www.firesafe.org.uk/fire-emergency-evacuation-plan-or-fire-procedure/. Last accessed 12th January 2016.

Gov.uk. (2015). Health protection – guidance Heatwave Plan for England. Available: https://www.gov.uk/government/publications/ heatwave-plan-for-england. Last accessed 12th January 2016.

Health and Safety Executive. (2011). Getting to grips with hoisting people. Available: http://www.hse.gov.uk/pubns/hsis3.pdf. Last accessed 12th January 2016.

Health and Safety Executive. (2012). Managing the risks from hot water and surfaces in health and social care. Available: http://www. hse.gov.uk/pubns/hsis6.pdf. Last accessed 12th January 2016.

National Institute for Health and Care Excellence. (2015). British National Formulary. Available: http://www.evidence.nhs.uk/formulary/bnf/current. Last accessed 12th January 2016.

National Institute for Health and Care Excellence. (2013). Falls in older people: assessing risk and prevention. Available: http://www.nice.org.uk/guidance/cg161/chapter/1-recommendations. Last accessed 12th January 2016.

National Institute for Health and Care Excellence. (2012). Healthcare-associated infections: prevention and control in primary and community care. Available: https://www.nice.org.uk/guidance/cg139/ifp/chapter/long-term-use-of-urinary-catheters. Last accessed 12th January 2016

National Institute for Health and Care Excellence. (2012). Identifying and managing complications in adults with type 1 diabetes. Available: http://pathways.nice.org.uk/pathways/type-1-diabetes-in-adults#path=view%3A/pathways/type-1-diabetes-in-adults/identifying-and-managing-complications-in-adults-with-type-1-diabetes.xml&content=view-in. Last accessed 12th January 2016

National Institute for Health and Care Excellence. (2011). Managing stable angina. Available: http://pathways.nice.org.uk/pathways/stable-angina#path=view%3A/pathways/stable-angina/managing-stable-angina.xml&content=view-node%3Anodes-providing-immediate-relief-and-short-term-prevention-of-angi. Last accessed 12th January 2016.

National Institute for Health and Care Excellence. (2014). Pressure ulcers: prevention and management. Available: https://www.nice.org.uk/guidance/cg179. Last accessed 12th January 2016.

UKHCA Guidance. (2012). Controlling Scalding Risks from Bathing and Showering. Available: http://www.ukhca.co.uk/pdfs/

BathingShowering.pdf#search="bathing". Last accessed 12th January 2016.

NHS England. (2011). Actions for End of Life Care: 2014-16. Available: https://www.england.nhs.uk/wp-content/uploads/2014/11/actions-eolc.pdf. Last accessed 12th January 2016.

NHS Choices. (2015). Hypothermia - Symptoms . Available: http://www.nhs.uk/Conditions/Hypothermia/Pages/Symptoms.aspx. Last accessed 12th January 2016.

Nursing & Midwifery Council. (2015). Standards for medicines management. Available: http://www.nmc.org.uk/standards/additional-standards/standards-for-medicines-management/. Last accessed 12th January 2016.

Nursing & Midwifery Council. (2015). The Code Professional standards of practice and behaviour for nurses and midwives. Available: http://www.nmc.org.uk/globalassets/sitedocuments/nmc-publications/revised-new-nmc-code.pdf. Last accessed 12th January 2016.

Stroke Assosiation. (2015). *Recognise The Signs of Stroke.* Available: https://www.stroke.org.uk/take-action/recognise-signs-stroke. Last accessed 15th January 2016.

About the Author

It was approximately seven months after qualifying as a nurse and gaining this time of experience on the wards that I got my first post in a care home. My first care plans took me a while to write, which prompted me to buy a little notebook. After thinking about different needs relating to the activities of daily living, I would write practice care plans using "***" as my patients' names. As the days and weeks went by, I found writing personalized care plans easier, and I became more efficient at keeping my patients' care notes up-to-date. It gives me the greatest pleasure sharing this with you, and I do hope that this book will provide some support during care planning.

Printed in Great Britain
by Amazon

29563232R00070